POTENTIALS OF DIGITALIZED INDIA

DR. JAGADEESH PILLAI

|| THE YOUTH OF INDIA – The Digital Minds ||

Contents

Contents

Acknowledgements

My sincere thanks to the enthusiastic young boy Anand J.S, who has helped me to find many students across the country and to interact with them to shape this book. He was there all along in every step to create this dream book.

My heartfelt thanks go to Iswarya J.S, the main editor of my book for her expertise and devotion while editing.

My love and regards to my son Pranav for helping in the process initial editing and re-arranging of chapters.

My deep appreciation goes to all of the others, here and there, who have made this book possible.

About The Author

Dr. Jagadeesh Pillai a voracious reader, Four Times Guinness World Record holder, writer, and true research scholar was born in Varanasi, the abode of Lord Shiva. He is Ph.D. in Vedic Science. He is a multi-faceted polymath with innate qualities, creative ideas and many remarkable achievements. Although his roots extend back to "Gods own Country"(Kerala), the residents of Varanasi feel proud of him and adore him as a child of Varanasi who caters to every individual in need without any expectations. A deep study into his profile reflects that he has added so many feathers to his cap which makes him quite unique. He is a four times Guinness Book of World Records Holder in the following subjects :

"Script to Screen" which he achieved by producing and directing a state of art animation film within the shortest time possible by breaking the earlier set record by Canadians. There are many national and international Awards and Recognitions to his credit.

Longest Line of Post Cards which he has done on the occasion of 163 years of Indian Postal Day by 16300 post cards. The event was also connected with a questionnaire about Indian Flag.

Largest Poster Awareness Campaign – This was achieved by designing an awareness campaign on the subject "Beti Bachao – Beti Padhao".

Largest Envelop – Towards tribute to Prime Minister's initiative 'Make in India' – he has created about 4000 sq meter envelop using waste papers.

Attempted by lighting 70000 candles on a 210 kg cake to celebrate the 70th Indian Independence day recorded in World Records India.

Attempted a documentary on Dhamek Stupa of Sarnath dubbing in 17 languages, result is waiting from Guinness World Records.

He is versatile in Gita teaching. The young generation is fond of his Gita teaching and he has changed the life of many young through his continued motivational boost up and teachings.

He has composed and sung Gayatri Mantra in 1000 different tunes.

He has composed and sung Hanuman Chalisa in 108 different tunes.

He has composed and sung hundreds of Sanskrit Bhajans, Patriotic songs, etc.

He has written and directed so many short films and documentaries for awareness campaigns.

He has done voluntary services to UP Police and Kerala Police to spread awareness campaigns on the various issue through videos and photography.

He is on the path of authoring thousands of books on Indian culture, Indian Temples, and the life of extraordinary people.

It is hard to believe that he has produced and directed more than 100 Documentaries on a particular city (Varanasi) which is done by a single person.

He has helped and guided more than 25 boys and girls to achieve world records through various creative and innovative methods.

A multifaceted person who can apply the best of his intellect using the God-given blessings which have been showered upon every human being granting them an immense capacity to learn, experience, and experiment with many things and do wonders in this world of discrimination and disparities.

He is a teacher and a student at the same time who always learns every day and teaches every day. As a master, his weakness was that he never sticks to a particular subject. Perhaps this weakness gives him the strength to master any area which he came across.

Each of his days dawned with learning a new topic and he spend most of his time experimenting and researching it.

He is also a selfless social activist and a motivational speaker.

His life was full of struggle, ups and downs, and failures. But he never gave up and faced all his trials and tribulations full of confidence. Today he is a successful young man with a lot of enthusiasm and rich life experience.

He has sung full Ram Charita Manas 51 hours audio by his own composition. He has also sung the whole Bhagavad-Gita in his own composition with a rhythmic background.

He has also sung "Lokah Samastha Sukhino Bhavantu" in 50 different languages.

Currently working on a detailed and scientific study on Veda, Upanishad, Puranas, Bhagavad Gita, etc.

Currently, he is the Hon' Chancellor of 'Eurasia Digital University'.

Awards

Four Times Guinness World Records

Winner of Mahatma Gandhi Vishwa Shanti Puraskar

Mahatma Gandhi Global Peace Ambassador
Kashi Ratna Award

Dr. APJ Abdul Kalam Motivational Person of the Year 2017

Mother Teresa Award

Indira Gandhi Priyadarshini Award

Bharat Vikas Ratna Award

Udyog Ratna Award

Vigyan Prasar Award

Poorvanchal Ratn Samman

Dr. Jagadeesh Pillai is a teacher of Vedic Science, Bhagavad Gita etc. Apart from this, he is also a Writer, Winger, Film Maker, Gemologist, Astro-Vastu Consultant, World Record Consultant, Pranic Healer, Spiritual Counsellor, Tarot Card reader etc.

He is the chairman of All India Malayali Association, Uttar Pradesh and also the National Secretary of 'Culture and Heritage' of the Indian Human Rights Association.

Foreword

FOREWORD

"Potentials of Digital India" by Dr Jagadeesh Pillai is an excellent literary work which describes the way our youth, especially the students respond to the Government of India's ambitious project – Digital India.

The effort that Dr Jagadeesh Pillai took for interacting and collecting opinions from students from across the country is truly amazing. His commitment and dedication is highly commendable.

I appreciate and admire him for this great work. It was such a great pleasure to see the brilliant responses from our young generation. Their foresight and vision of the digital revolution can be realized by reading this book. I have now strong faith in the future of our nation because the students of the new era are having high dreams, thoughts and imagination and technologically influenced to do innovations which will enable them to make our country proud in the near future.

I strongly believe that this is the first time that an author has made a nation-wide campaign to identify what the young minds/students expect from one of the most prestigious projects of the government, collect their responses and made it into a book.

I am running short of words to describe it. I am sure that this book will be a huge success. I wish you all the success of for your future endeavours as well.

Adv. Rajesh Panayantatta
Suprement Court
New Delhi

Preface

First of all let me say, this book is the result of my passion to interact, nourish, and encourage young minds of the country. I always feel energetic and excited to communicate with the students. Their views, opinions, suggestions and queries reflected their strong thinking capacity and will power.

It was one fine day in Banaras that I randomly thought about various projects which are being implemented by the government. But I constantly used to see the term "Digital India" in social media, magazines, newspapers, articles etc. I began to wonder about its great significance. I had a thorough study on it and was mesmerized by the development and transformation that it aspires to give to our country and its citizens.

An intuition came to my mind to write a book about it. But there are already many books based on Digital India. Then how will I make my book unique? That time, just like Archimedes's "Eureka" moment, an idea came to my mind, and I decided to interact with the youth across the country, and to ask them their opinions, views for the potential of Digital India and to make a book from that.

I don't postpone things for the next day. So the same day itself I started preparing the questions to be asked in order to understand their vision and foresight of Digital India. I contacted my friends and relatives from all over the country and received guidance and suggestions from many. I personally interacted with students and discussed about various aspects of Digital India. I noted down their points. Their views and suggestions are included in the book. While reading their views, you will be amazed to know the aspirations, dreams and the strong thinking ability of our young minds.

The tremendous support I received and the enthusiasm they showed, motivated me to overcome all the obstacles and complete this book on time.

Dr. Jagadeesh Pillai

INTRODUCTION

Digital India!

What comes to your mind when you hear this word?

The mission and outcome of this project itself is a magnificent dream for us, right? It is not just a dream now; in a few years you can see our country giving a tough competition in development to many countries. Our country is fast progressing and in order to make it much brilliant, Prime Minister Shri. Narendra Modi has launched "Digital India" on July 2nd 2015.

The depth and quality of thinking of the children of the current generation are entirely different from that of the previous generation. During the 90's, children had very little access to the television and many other things for their entertainment, communication as well as for improving their knowledge. Mobile phone was an alien thing for the majority. The condition is not like that now. Even a 3 year old child knows how to unlock an iPhone. This is the impact of technology on our generation. The younger ones know many technological things than their predecessors. They are grown up in an advanced technological environment. So, they are accustomed to grasp information's easily.

Our world is rapidly advancing and IT has a major role in it. Every nation should create better infrastructure in digital sector in order to walk its path in development. Digital India is a programme aimed to transform our country into a digitally empowered society and knowledge economy. "Digital India" has 9 pillars:-

1. Broadband Highways

2. Universal Access to mobile connectivity

3. Public internet access program

4. E-Governance: Reforming government through technology

5. E-Kranti: Electronic delivery of Services

6. Information for all

7. Electronics Manufacturing

8. IT for Jobs

9. Early harvest programmes

This book is a first-hand view of what our young Indians, the students of our nation; feel about our government's revolutionary project "Digital India". Various aspects of Digital India were discussed with a number of students across the country of the age group 20-30. This book is the result of the reviews, aspirations, foresight and visions they have in mind for Digital India. It is a small support to show gratitude to my nation by showcasing the relevance of such a wonderful initiative "Digital India".

Hope this book gives the readers an in-depth view and a multi-dimensional perspective of India's most ambitious project for digital revolution.

PM's Vision to Digital India

These words truly are filled with commitment, dedication and the desire to make our country digitally sufficient and developed. As we all know our Prime Minister Shri. Narendra Modi is a "Man of Action" and he delivers his promises.

At the launch of Digital India in Delhi, he said that he had several visions towards the Digital India initiative.He said that these are his dreams about the project.

He dreamed of a digital India,

Where high-speed "Digital Highways" unite the nation...

Where 1.2 billion connected Indians drive Innovation...

Where knowledge is strength – and empowers the people...

Where access to information knows no barrier...

Where the government is open and governance

transparent...

Where technology ensures the citizen-government interface is incorruptible

Where government services are easily and efficiently available to citizens on mobile devices...

Where the government proactively engages with the people through social media.. where quality education reaches the most inaccessible corners driven by digital learning...

Where quality healthcare percolates right up to the remotest regions powered by e-Healthcare..

Where the farmers are empowered with real-time information to be connected with global markets...

Where mobile enabled emergency services ensure personal security...

Where cyber security becomes an integral part of our national security...

Where mobile and e-Banking ensures financial inclusion...

Where e-Commerce drives entrepreneurship...

Where the World looks to India for the next big idea...

Where the citizen is an empowered citizen.

All these vision statements are not just dreams, but the government is working hard round the clock to make it a reality. We can see that the Digital India program is doing a phenomenal work in transforming our lives.

CHAPTER TWO

Support to Digital India

It is a revolutionary initiative from our government and it has immense potential and we can undoubtedly say that it will make our country to reach the zenith of development.

As responsible citizens, it is our duty to support and contribute towards programmes which aim to build our nation. Whether it's about improving the literacy rate or creating job opportunities, we should focus only on the positive aspects of it.

Most of my friends do share their views that the Digital India initiative by the government will make our country and its citizens more productive.

Digitally self reliable is what our country needs to become now. It's happening slowly. That is also a positive sign. See, slowly the citizens are learning and understanding the vast potentials and possibilities of digital services. In old days people were afraid of even doing online transactions, because they felt that it's not safe. But the atmosphere has been changing slowly. Now more and more people are doing e-services in their daily life. For example, paying electricity bills online, paying phone bills online, booking movie-bus-train and flight tickets online etc.

The Digital India initiative will improve the National Optic Fibre Network (NOFN), and it has set a new broadband connectivity to 250000 Gram Panchayats by the end of 2017. It will help the government to interact with the people of those regions and they can be provided with necessary services.

More awareness should be created about the great advantages that the digital services offer. Then we will have majority of the citizens shifting to digital services rather than the traditional modes.

Digital divide will slowly be eliminated. The younger generations of India is wholeheartedly supporting and is wishing to see that our country is prospering and developing in all aspects, especially in Digital infrastructure.

CHAPTER THREE

Digital India & Women Empowerment

There is no doubt about it. Indian women are developing, so does India! The status or level of development of a society can be measured by the condition of the women in that particular society. Women have active role in shaping the future of our country just like men. Women can make use of the digital services to improve their skills, knowledge and education and it also helps them to earn necessary income for their livelihood.

More than the urban women, Digital India aims at improving the social and economic life style of the rural women. Digital India aims at providing mobile connectivity and broadband to 2.5 lakh villages by 2019.Mobile and internet will be the backbone of this revolution. Through skill development, the task can be effectively completed. The best example of interlinking Technology is an initiative called "Internet Saathi" long term vision of Shri. Ratan Tata.

Shri. Ratan Tata along with tech giant Intel and Google has joined on a mission to help rural Indian women to access the internet. It will help them to learn new things and also help them to do jobs and earn a living. Only a few populations have access to internet in rural and remote regions and Digital India aims to bring them to the circle of connectivity also. "Internet Saathi" program by Google will give around 1000 specially manufactured bicycles with internet connected devices. It will give the women easy and convenient access to the internet and its services. The programme will be launched across 4,500 villages of Gujarat, Jharkhand, Rajasthan in a few months. It is expected to reach approximately half a million rural women. It will also lead to bridge the technology gender divide prevailing in the country.

The W2E2 (Wireless Women For Entrepreneurship & Empowerment), was a revolutionary program which was launched in 2014.Around 10 women were selected from each location. Total they choose 5 locations from 4 states. They were selected from various self help groups working in different fields.

They were given training in computer hardware, OS and software basics, internet and the use of components like keyboards, cpu, mouse, monitor etc. They were given 6 months of training. After half the training period, they are provided with a Google assisted program known as "HWGO" (Helping Women Go Online) where they are trained to use internet and basic computer knowledge.

The main aim of this is to empower women and make them more skilled and talented in the field of Internet and communications, making them better entrepreneurs and thereby their socio-economic development will happen.

There are also many such NGO's which are very active in improving the life standard of women, especially rural women. Active support from the government also acts as an integral part.

Top performing Village Level Entrepreneurs (VLE'S), were felicitated and awarded the title "Digital India Women's Champions" by Ministry of Electronics and Information Technology at New Delhi. Such events will further help more women to overcome their family and societal barriers to become successful entrepreneurs. Every single woman can act like a ray of hope for millions of women across the country.

CHAPTER FOUR

Digital India and Scope of Employment

One of the main problems which our country faces today is unemployment. It's a negative thing which hinders our growth and progress of our country and this should be seriously taken care of. The Digital India programme is multi-dimensional one and aims to solve many issues like unemployment, education related issues, etc.

According to the calculations and expectations of the government, The Digital India expects to generate approximately 50 million job opportunities. The mission of the government is to create a link between Digital-Skill and Make in India projects which will eventually create millions of job opportunities. This will eliminate the issue of unemployment up to a large extent.

The Digital India programme will improve the service delivery mechanisms and infrastructure facilities of the government and its institutions. To be exact, it is estimated that around 50 million citizens of our great nation will be directly or indirectly benefitted as a result of Digital India.

Once this mission of Digital India is completed, the literacy rate of the citizens will increase, unemployment will be brought down, the lifestyle and status of the citizens will improve and a lot more good things will happen. I am sure that the Digital India programme will helps to use the tremendous possibility of our nation's human resources and use it towards its development and prosperity.

CHAPTER FIVE

Advancement in Current Educational System

Digital India and its projects will boost up the educational sector along with other sectors like industry, commerce etc.

Digital India aims to make our entire country digitally connected in a short span of 4 years. As we all know digital divide is a serious problem especially in developing countries. Through Digital India, there will be tremendous push towards educating the citizens in the digital field and this in turn results in the generation of citizens who are skilled, educated and socially and economically developed. A digitally literate citizen can be a productive asset for our country.

Digital India project also aims at connecting all the schools across the country with broadband and Wi-Fi connectivity. It also gives importance for MOOC (Massive Open Online

Courses), through which the citizens can learn a variety of subjects and courses online. This will help the students particularly from rural areas in particular to get quality education which will help them to brighten up their future.

Through e-libraries, the students can read hundreds and thousands of books online for free, from their computer or mobile devices. This will help them to improve their subject knowledge and also to learn new things. Boosting E-learning is the main area where the Digital India project aims to give the citizens a positive boost in their educational qualifications.

I am pretty sure that with the passage of time, the Digital India initiative will give successful results in improving the educational status of our countrymen.

Digital India program helps the school as well as college students' indiverse ways. It will improve the way the students learn their lessons. It will bring a huge revolution in the academic sector. The introuduction of e-learning and e-libraries will give the students improved learning mechanisms which will help them to learn a variety of new and innovative things.

Digital libraries will help the students to easily access millions of books online easily.It will help the students to refer them and gain precious knowledge.It will make them even more qualified, skilled and talented.

Creation of a knowledge based society is one of the aims of Digital India. Technology driven methods of education will positively affect the depth of learning as well as the output of the students. New, systematic and innovative methods of learning will make learning process very student friendly.

E-basta is one project which supports the government's Digital India initiative and e-learning. Through e-basta, school text books can be accessed in digital format and can be viewed from laptops or smart phones.

The most important thing about introuction of IT and Digital India initiatives in edcuational sector is accessing of educational resources from remote areas through the use of internet directly from their homes.

CHAPTER SIX

New Business Possibilitie

The Digital India programme will create many new business possibilities. I have got many reasons to believe so.

The e-Commerce industry in our country is rapidly developing. And this is also a factor which contributes towards the revenue earned through postal services (delivery of goods bought and sold online).

Digital India will push the investments in IT and its allied services in a whole new level. This will eventually improve the IT sector and will also generate large number of employment opportunities.

In future if the global IT market is experiencing a downfall, The Indian IT firms can make the best out of the opportunity through Digital India programme. The growth and development of digital services will offer millions of job opportunities. Innovation and rapid development will also boost the growth in job opportunities.

Digital India gives business opportunities in agriculture, telecom sector, finance, marketing, infrastructure etc. and the best thing is that through these revolutionary programmes we aim to reduce our IT imports to 0, which means becoming self sufficient in IT and electronics manufacturing.

Digital marketing (Marketing products and services using digital platform) has become the job of the decade. Skilled Digital M specialists are hard to find and there is a huge demand for them. Because, in this digital era, for a company to survive they should make their presence felt in the online world.

Tech giants like Facebook and Google are launching their campus centres in India and it will provide thousands of job opportunities for our people. New and diverse methods of doing business will emerge and as a result the overall industry will have diverse growth opportunities.

CHAPTER SEVEN

Impact on Literacy Rate

The Digital India initiative is going to be a grand success and its activities will eventually have a positive impact on the literacy rate of our citizens.

It will have a great impact on the literacy rate of our country. Digital India and its projects will tremendously boost the educational background and infrastructure of our citizens. More and more learning options will be available for our citizens.

Especially online courses like MOOC. Through an internet enabled computer or a mobile phone, a person can learn and get various educational information. Distance education through online has now become a popular mode of education especially for students of rural areas. It will benefit those students of remote areas who lack the access to transportation facilities and who cannot afford the huge expense. These students can make use of internet and get a wide range of educational options even while sitting at their homes.

E-Pathahala was introduced by MHRD (Ministry Of Human Resources) to promote learning. Under this scheme, NCERT books of classes 1 to 12 can be freely accessed. And it is available in both Hindi and English. Its mobile application can be downloaded in all major platforms like Android, ios and Windows.

E-learning is the main advantage of Digital India for students. Smart classrooms, e-libraries etc. will also boost the educational level, skill and quality of our younger generation. As a result, we will have a generation of top class skilled professionals who will take our country forward to the path of glory.

Most of the youngsters believe that there will be a positive change in the literacy rate of our country in the next 5 years of the launch of Digital India campaign, because positive signs can be seen in the initial stages also. Digital India also gives strong focus on improving the educational condition of the citizens through digital technologies.

E-classrooms and E-libraries will be great benefits for the students who can easily refer millions of books online for free and also listen to video lessons from teachers across the globe. Even students living in rural areas can use these facilities. The government aims to build more digital infrastructure especially in rural areas. Internet will be made available to people living in rural areas also.

As a result for those who cannot get enough transport facilities to go to schools or colleges can easily learn day to day lessons by sitting at home. MOOC's (Massive Open

Online Courses) and Distance Education through Internet are becoming common nowadays. Thus, the youth in particular are getting a variety of learning options which will help them to improve their skills, knowledge and productivity. As a result, the qualified students will easily get job opportunities and the issue of unemployment can be solved.

CHAPTER EIGHT

Reduced Documentation & Digi-Locker

Digi-Locker is one of Digital India's programmes, which allows the citizens to store their documents such as driving license, Aadhar card, electoral id and certificates in pdf/ image format on a public cloud space and making them available at any required moment. This helps in eliminating the use of paper documents. The citizens can create a verified Digi-Locker facility by using their Aadhar card number (UIDAI Number).The citizens can also upload to their Digi-Locker account, a variety of other documents too. And these can be verified using electronic or e-sign facility.

Digi-Locker has many advantages:

It will eliminate the burden of paper documents. As the certificates can be retrieved in electronic form, tremendous amount of paper use and its wastage can be avoided. It will save our planet as well.

The documents can be retrieved from any part of the world. It will be made available from the cloud storage anytime, anywhere.

It can also be signed electronically (e-sign)

Digi-Locker gives everyone 1GB of space for storing their documents. This is sufficient for saving a person's documents. As these are scanned files /pdf's, it will not consume much storage space. It will be a life saver for travellers who usually take many copies of their original documents for verification purposes during their journey.

It is very simple process to register. You can also do it using your Smartphone. Just download the "Digi-Locker" application from Android Play store. Add your phone number validate your account with your Aadhar card number and follow the instructions.

CHAPTER NINE

Digital Revolution and Services

Digital India is one spectacular initiative which is going to boost the Digital Revolution in our country. It has countless advantages which aim to make our country and its people more developed and productive.

Digital services are a great relief, especially for those who live in rural areas. They can get access to a world of possibilities through digital services.

We can see the advantages of digital services in our daily life. Traditional methods of services are being overtaken by digital services which are far more convenient, safe, secure, reliable and fast!

The Digital India is a massive project worth billions of rupees. The investment will come back as monetary and non-monetary profits in the form of developments of the citizens and also in the way of development of the nation. This initiative makes the citizen's life more comfortable, making services more effective, secure, safe and transparent and also creating job opportunities. Digital India is really a game changer!

In less than 5 years we can see the positive impacts that the Digital India initiative made. The young Indians strongly believe that it will be historic outcome which will change the way the world see our country and its citizens.

There are countless number of advantages for digital services.These advantages makes our daily lifes even more simple, convenient and meaningful.These services are being introduced in a variety of sectors and are doing very well in improving and transforming the lifes of citizens.

It is relatively fast, secure, prompt and convenient to use.

Helps to save cost, time and resources.

Helps to reduce the use of paper and also to conserve nature.

Services can be accessible from any part of the globe, 24 x7 and 365 days a year.

Gives the people of remote areas to access information and other services.

Makes our day to day life more efficient.

Students get multiple options of learning and make learning friendlier.

Safe and quick financial transactions can be possible.

More development options will be available for villages and rural areas.

Innovation and technology will create new and improved machineries which improve the method of production leading to the manufacturing of quality products.

Patients can refer the internet and learn more information about the diseases.

Enables fast and high definition communication facilities.

Common citizens can make use of all the available resources and take part in the digital revolution.We have billions of mobile connections, huge internet user base also. More number of people are now using digital transactions in their day to day purposes.

People who have enough knowledge about these services should spend some time to encourage people to use digital services who still follow traditional methods, and if one person helps another one and gives him awareness and explains to him about its uses, imagine what will happen when millions of us decide to do so? Millionsof people can be taught about the use of such services, and then it will do wonders.

CHAPTER TEN

Rebuilding of Social and Economic Sectors

Having a well diversified and strong digital Infrastructure and facilities in the country will help to address many social and economic issues. And it will also help to rebuild the socio-economic condition of the country as well.

We are now undergoing a mass movement towards digitally developed nation. Our communication systems and satellites are globally recognised as the best in the world. Our society and countrymen should rise up to the expectations.

Socio – economic development will happen when a country is getting strong in its digital infrastructure. People will get more educational opportunities, more employment options, wide areas of knowledge can be gained and so on. Even the people of remote areas can get access to many services through internet.

Socio-Economic issues will gradually get reduced when a nation develops. Once the nation develops, it will have enough technology and resources to tackle its problems. Unemployment and poverty being the most concerned issues, through Digital India, there will be tremendous job opportunities, enormous amount of learning options etc. which will help the citizens to be more productive and to improve their socio-economic conditions.

CHAPTER ELEVEN

Benefits to Common Citizens

A lot of services like tax, bill payments, passport etc. are processed online. It has benefitted the life of the common citizens in a number of ways. Let's take the example of Passport services.

Many years back, as we all know after applying for the passport in the passport office we had to wait for months to get the application processed. The delivery of the passport to the applicant also takes months'. Think about the situation now; anyone can apply for the passport online, get the application processed in a few days, and get an appointment date. The person can go to the passport office to complete the verification process and it's done! How simple the system has become!

Many traditional services will be made available in a digitalised manner. As a result, the system will be accessible to people on the go. Now, people can pay bills, transfer money, book tickets for trains, buses, flights, movies etc simply using internet as a medium using their PC, laptops or mobile phones. We no longer have to stand in long queues to get those services. Using Digi-Locker, people can now store their documents and id/driving licence/pan card etc. on cloud storage and can retrieve it from anywhere, anytime. You don't need to carry copies of documents any longer! That's how time and technology flies as a result of digitalisation.

I personally believe that the common citizens will benefit a lot as a result of this great programme called Digital India. My firm support for this initiative which will have amazing benefits for the citizens of my nation.

CHAPTER TWELVE

Social and Economic Development

Digital India will truly be revolutionary factor which will 100 percent improve the socio-economic condition of our country. Socio-Economic development of the citizens can be improved through various schemes and programmes of Digital India.

It gives the citizens of our country immense opportunities to learn, grow and develop their skills and potentials. Once we have a generation of talented and skilled human beings, any socio-economic issues can be systematically solved.

Digital India will create millions of job opportunities, and eventually unemployment and poverty related issues will be gradually reduced. More than 4.5 lakh crore is the proposed investments in Digital India promised by the top industrialists which includes business tycoons like Mukesh Ambani, Sunil Mittal etc. Google has already started installing free Wi-Fi hotspots (Rail Wire) in more than 400 railway stations across the country.

Digital India will help to improve transparency and to

eliminating corruption. Some time back, for submitting an application or a complaint, people were forced to give bribes to the government officials. Now, since everything can be done online, exploitation from such employees and middlemen had been eliminated. It makes our public services more efficient.

CHAPTER THIRTEEN

IT Revolution towards Economic Development

Jobs! Development! And Growth! – are the things which will bring revolution in IT field. Digital India will kick off the next round of Digital Revolution in our country and it is going to be spectacular than ever.

Digital India aims at making our country digitally developed and strong, by making our digital infrastructure strong and our citizens digitally connected. I think, it is not just a government programme but a massive revolution. And I am sure that it will create tons and thousands of jobs and will boost the development of our country and its people.

IT or Information Technology is among the rapidly growing industry which creates countless number of job opportunities. Through the advancements in science, technology and innovation, this sector is making a huge leap forward. It also helps in transforming the life of people in a variety of ways.

Providing mobile and internet facilities for rural people, especially women will make great transformation in their life. It will also help the government to reach out to them and provide them with variety of facilities.

In the present era of Digital technology, if a nation wants to progress and achieve development, then it should have a well established digital infrastructure.

The initial stage of Digital India campaign has started showing great positive responses as it has created many success stories. More and more citizens started using the enormous possibilities of digital services and transactions, which is a good sign that our people have understood the advantages of it. It is a clear indication that our country is about to make wonders in the Digital world.

CHAPTER FOURTEEN

Necessity of an initiative like Digital India

Practically speaking, we are already late. See, many countries which got independence after 1947, are now fully developed countries. They framed and implemented projects through the technological advancements. We are very late in implementing project like Digital India.

We should wholeheartedly thank Prime Minister Shri. Narendra Modi Ji for bringing up this fantastic project – Digital India - for our country. It will make our country #1, once the project is successfully completed. Signs of it can be felt in our day to day life. Many people now use internet for many service like paying bills, booking tickets etc. That is a good sign that the government's mission is getting successful.

When a good portion of the people will start using digital services, rest of the population will follow it gradually.

Massive developments in the country will happen as a result of Digital India. It will create many job opportunities and will also help to eradicate many social problems like unemployment and poverty. As a result the society and our economic conditions will improve. Digital India is one such initiative which will make our country in the path of development.

Hope we will see the launch of such projects like this in our near future, which will further improve the lives of the citizens of our country.

Digital India – Possible Outcomes Expected

Whatever be the outcome, I am sure of one thing that it will be great for our country and our citizens. The numbers of people who use traditional modes of services are gradually decreasing and there is a sudden rise in the number of digital service users.

Application of digital systems for various day to day activities had made our daily life more simple and comfortable. Traditional methods consumed much time, more cost and effort.

There are many positive impacts for the Digital India and its programmes. I strongly believe that it will create diversified job opportunities, reduce the burden of documentation, help to solve the issue of poverty and deal with many other economic as well as social issues that our country faces. These are the factors which hinders our growth opportunities. Once these are eliminated, then our country can strongly achieve its developmental goals.

The main advantage of the Digital India programme is that it will create a nation which is rich in digital sector. Our IT and electronics industry will prosper and eventually we can be self sufficient in electronic manufacturing. It will improve the quality and standard of the citizens. Thereby our nation will prosper in many fields. Now almost every application, whether its passport or for some government exams, all can be applied online. It helps to save paper and nature, because, even for an exam registration, usually the form consists of 3-4 pages. Imagine that a candidate applies for 20 exams in a year, which means, he/she had used about 60 papers. Since it can be done online, those 60 papers can be saved. Just think the number of applicants for various exams/other services alone, imagine the huge number of papers and the trees which can be saved.

We can even book LPG cylinders and pay tax returns online. We can now use e-hospital facility to book appointments to premier hospitals in the country like All India Institute of Medical Science and National Institute of Mental Health & Neuro Sciences online. The patient needs to register it using his Aadhar number. The process of registration and fixing appointment are very easy and simple to perform.

As a result of Digital India scheme, we will have improved IT and Communication networks, optimum utilisation of our resources can be possible, and it also makes many traditional services easier to perform and implement. Improved digital infrastructure and connectivity and delivery of services in digital form will transform the life of every person in the country.

CHAPTER SIXTEEN

Security Threats and IT sector

I believe what many people feel about IT or digital sector is that "it is not safe". This attitude should change. And there is also a high growth in people who use online transactions. It is a clear sign that they had overcome their "fear" and started using online portals.

Earlier, majority of the people thought that online transactions and activities are tough to do, and are not so safe and so on. The confusions were endless. Through the introduction of Digital India, a vast portion of the people in our country started adopting themselves to the growing digital atmosphere.

We can see people nowadays moving towards cashless transactions, using internet as a medium for accessing government services, payment of bills, booking tickets for flights-buses-trains-movies etc. This is truly a dramatic change! Earlier, we all know, it was not like this.

The main thing that most people hesitate to do online features is the fear of losing privacy and security issue.

The technology must be utilised for creating new and advanced methods, for protecting the digital services, especially against spamming, hacking, online frauds etc. In newspapers, we can see a lot of reports and cases of online frauds and security problems. Issues and reports like this will further create tensions and misunderstandings about the credibility of digital services and will make the general public afraid to use such services.

So we should have a strong mechanism to protect the digital services and to track the violators. Then the people will have more courage and trust to use the digital services more.

Talking about security drawbacks, online frauds are the most commonly seen crime in the digital world. It includes cheating for monetary and non-monetary gains. Both are considered as punishable and criminal offences.

There should be well equipped and systematic security systems to tackle such issues. Nowadays there are highly equipped systems to identify and capture the violators or criminals in the online world. So there is no need to worry about the safety issue. We just have to be careful about your actions in the online world. Just like the proverb says, "Prevention is always better than cure".

Understanding about various threats and its causes is very important. It will make the users more conscious. Privacy is an important matter. There are many instances where the photos of individuals are misused by others. A main reason is the over influence of social media. People upload their photos and moments on social media without any hesitation. Keep one thing in mind that whatever we put on the internet, it will be available to anyone on the planet! There is high chance that somebody will misuse it.

There are few steps which will help us in making the digital world, a safe place.

Do not share any personal details on social media, whether its photos, numbers or contact details.

Avoid interactions with strangers.

Never store financial details in your phone or computers.

Keep passwords complex, and use "space" bars in the passwords.

Use updated anti-virus software.

All these measures will help to maintain security in the online world. Even though there are mass digital revolution and the tremendous growth and development in digital world, we must be careful about these security issues. So we can be safe from being cheated.

Banking Sector

Banking and finance sector will see abundant amount of transformation under Digital India programme.Net banking and cashless transactions are taking over traditional banking methods. Net Banking or Intenet banking is one of the most amazing things which happened in the banking industry as a result of this IT revolution.Net banking means doing banking transactions (receiving and transfering funds) online using internet as a medium.Understanding its convenience and simplicity, people are now shifting to e-banking rather than traditional banking methods.

E-banking is safe, secure, and amazingly fast! The main advantage is that the flow of funds can be tracked and it will be easy to identify those who have unhealthy and suspicious transactions. E-banking enables the customers to experience their banking in a more convenient and smooth way.

It is easier to perform, convenient, and really fast. Nowadays almost every bank now has their own net banking web portals which allows customers to log in to it using their respective user id and password, and can use regular banking features and much more.

The government has given licenses to few payments banks like Paytm, Airtel etc., and this will be a revolutionary step in our finance sector. More and more e-commerce platforms are coming up because now a day's people concentrate more on buying and selling goods and services online.

In the past, all the customers got the same services and plans, but now due to technological advancements and competition, the banks provide their customers with customisable plans and services which suit the interests and necessities of the customers.

E-banking has another advantage. We can block our account instantly, if we find some suspicious activity in our account or if our credit/debit card had been lost. Funds cannot be moved from the account thereafter.

Almost every bank in the country has net banking, mobile banking services and applications. Competition and threat of new entrants force the banks to create new and advanced features of services in order to maintain its customer base and also to attract new customers. Even passbooks are now available as e-passbooks, and bank statements can be retrieved from net banking. So now unlike old days, there is no reason to practically go to the bank and stand in long queues to get your passbook printed, or to transfer money to another account.

Traditional banking can be done only when the bank

branch is open. But the main advantage is that net banking facility is available 24x7, anywhere in the globe. The user can send money, transfer funds, pay bills, book tickets for movies,flights,buses,trains, purchase goods etc. using this facility.Funds can be transferred to anyone on the globe instantly.Earlier it took much time to do so using regular banking methods.

Digital India can further improve the net banking facilities. Innovative features and services can be added to the banking facilities which will improve the quality of banking as a whole.

Now banks have started self account creation facilities using their bank's app. Which means, customers can create an account in the bank using their mobile phones by entering their information like aadhar card details,election id details, PAN number etc. on the bank's mobile application. In areas where there are no bank branches are available, this facility will help the people to use banking services from their mobile devices.Due to this, financial inclusion will happen in a rapid pace. Hence the under privileged section of people will also get an opportunity in doing financial services.

Digital India will further make the banking sector and its functions more advanced and user friendly for the customers.

Benefits to Senior Citizens

Digital India programme is not only for the youth but it also gives due consideration for the betterment of life of the elderly population as well. They can also reap many benefits. Through Digital India programmes each and every citizen of India could be connected around the world. Free flow of communication will happen between family relations or with friends. Even people living in remote areas will have access to communication facilities and internet.

Various governmental services can be performed online. So these aged people need not go out, travel and stand in long queues. They can use these services directly from their homes. Digital India and its various programmes will further improve the lifestyle of the older generations. It will make their living convenient and simple.

They can also get access to a lot of day to day services online. They can use the internet to communicate with their loved ones, listen to news and current affairs around the globe, make easy fund transfers (bank transactions), and pay bills and so on.

E-hospital system launched now, allows patients to book appointments to major hospitals in the country like AIIMS. It is a great advantage for people, especially people of old age groups. They can sit at their homes and book appointments. They no longer need to visit the hospitals and stand in long queues for getting appointments.

As a result of Digital India, their daily lives have become more convenient.

CHAPTER NINETEEN

Impacts on Commerce and Business

Commerce and business will see tremendous growth as a result of Digital India. It will have a great impact on our IT exports and e-commerce industry in particular.

It will create new and improved methods for doing business, and as a result there will be a boost in the trade sector. More and more firms will enter the market utilising the golden opportunities. This will further enable competition and will improve the quality of products and services. Prices will be stabilised and it will be a great benefit for the customers as well.

Making digital payments is far more safe and comfortable than traditional payment methods. Nowadays there are many government projects which gives support to start an enterprise/firms/start up's. And the firms can be registered online. Digital India is changing the overall environment of doing business.

The Jan Dhan Yojana has helped out to improve financial

inclusion. Millions of poor people, who never had a bank account, have opened bank accounts through this scheme. This had improved business transactions through banks.

Our country is the second largest tclecom market in the world and it is the third country with the largest number of internet users. According to various financial analysts, the Digital India campaign will boost Gross Domestic Product (GDP) of our country up to $ 1 trillion by the end of 2025. Foreign Direct Investment (FDI) has also increased and more and more national as well as international firms are coming to invest in our country seeing the golden opportunities in the commerce sector.

Digital Start-up Firms

Start up firm is a newly launched business firm which offers innovative product or service.After the introduction of Digital India and Startup India, there is huge growth in the number of start up firms. The government gives all the support, including financial support for starting a start up.It leads to the creation of new and innovative products.It creates many job opportunities also.

They get a lot of benefits from the goverment like:

Tax exception for a few years.

Easy registration process.

Start up fests will be conducted, which gives the start up entrepreneurs many opportunities to meet the investors across the globe.

Easy availability of credit.The government will give enough and more support for startups.A sum of 10,000 crore has been allotted by the government to the developmet of startups.

Start-up ventures have great scope for further development and expansion. They have now become the next choice for professional/management students. We have more and more youths in particular, coming up with very brilliant ideas, which had gained much appreciation from tech giants like Microsoft and Google. Just like our Prime Minister said, "We have many problems but we also have 1 billion minds to solve it."

Innovations and new ideas will boost the way the start up's performing and it will also lead our country to solve many socio economic problems also.

CHAPTER TWENTY-ONE

Improvements in IT Service

Our Prime Minister Narendra Modi once said "I dream of a Digital India, where government is open and governance is transparent".

I think that the government has already focusing on that, because, many government services can now be done online. Whether it's applying for a vacancy/exam/passport, booking gas cylinders, paying electricity and water bills, etc, all of these can now be done online. The standards of the common citizen have improved.

Without the intervention of various intermediaries, the citizens can directly obtain necessary services from the government, and this had gradually reduced corruption and eradicated the delays in receiving the services.

The wonderful thing is that we can even share our ideas/opinions /complaints to the Prime Minister through his web portal mygov.in/writetopm. That is truly an amazing thing. I have read a lot about people sharing their opinions and getting responses from the Prime Minister himself. See how wonderful democracy has become.

The exploitations by the officers and bureaucrats have been gradually declined because the citizens can now get what they need directly from the government. Signs of good governance are being seen in majority of the government offices and services.

CHAPTER TWENTY-TWO

Digital Divide

Digital Divide/Digital Split, is the discrepancy between the people who have access and knowledge about digital services (like the internet) and those who have not.

This is an issue in developing countries in particular. This should be carefully dealt with. There are many factors which affectsuch a divide, economic-political conditions, age, income, family conditions etc.

Attempts are already on the move to bridge this gap, and the government is doing a wonderful job by providing more opportunities to learn about digital services, providing digital infrastructure for those who do not have it etc.These are ways through which the problem can be solved. In many countries even in developed ones, digital divide is a serious issue.

By the revolutionary project like Digital India, I am sure that it will help a lot to reduce this gap. Nowadays, smartphones are avaibale at a very cheap price, and as a result even the poor and common people can now use internet and other digital services.This will help to bridge the gap of digital divide.

The DSA (Digital Saksharta Abhiyan) aims to provide training in digital area for an estimated 5.2 million people by the end of 2018.Such programmes will help more and more people to get trained to use digital services and its various applications.

Giving internet and digital equipmets at subsidised rates will help the low income groups an opportunity to get these services. The students will be given high quality computer and IT education from the LP school level itself, it will be a great method to solve digital divide.

CHAPTER TWENTY-THREE

Digital India Campaign

I don't think that anyone in their right mindset will ever say that Digital India is a curse! It is a marvellous conceptto transform our country into a digitally empowered nation.It is an initiative to lead our country to a provide "Digital Literacy". It will be a spectacular initiative that will do wonders in many areas. It will give countless advantages to our country in different fields, whether its communication, business, service or industry.

Digital India is not just a normal government project, but a massive movement which is going to change the course of our country.Rapid economic growth will surely happen. There are tons of benefits, I would like to mention some of them:

1. It will transform the way we use a variety of daily services.It will improve our convenience, saves our time and money.

2. More and more citizens will have access to digital connectivity.

3. It will help to create new and improved methods for perosnal security and as a result there will be gradual decrease in crime rates.

4. Students in remote areas can also get access to rich source of information through e-learning and e-libraries.

5. Citizens can avail a variety of government services by sitting at their homes.

6. Cashless transactions will be used more, so cash flow in the economy can be maintained.

7. E-governance will improve the way the citizens and the government agencies interact with each other.It will eliminate the over influence and delays created by middlemen.

8. The online businesses will propser and more and more start up firms will enter the market.It will solve the issue of unemployment also.

There are also many other countless number of advantages that will show up once this project reaches its full swing. Considering all these, I believe the Digital India campaign is truly a boon for our country and its citizens.

CHAPTER TWENTY-FOUR

Digital India and its Challenges

The main challenge will be to make people adapt to the digital environment. Majority of the people are used to doing the traditional methods and they should be made aware of how to transform and adapt themselves to the digital ways of doing things. This is a herculean task, but it is possible through awareness campaigns and making the common people understand the benefits of digital services.

Once they start using it, then they will realise its good sides.Then they feel it comfortable to use it in their day to day lifes. Security concerns and lack of knowledge about it are the reasons why people normally hesitate to do it.This attitude will change in the course of time when they are made aware about its advanatges and good qualities.

The other challenge is the political factors.When the governement launches some project for the betterment of the nation, then everyone should support it.But that is not happening now.There is a protest for each and everything.Government implements projects as a solution for various socio-economic issues and to make our lives even more comfortable.

This unhealthy mindset of some people by political competition must be changed,atleast for the sake of our country.Everyone should have one mission in their mind – our nation's progress and we should only focus on that.

CHAPTER TWENTY-FIVE

Health Sectors

Unlike any other digital projects, the Digital India gives due consideration to the health sector too. With enough and more technologies in hand, It gives the health sector an opportunity to equally grow and develop just like other industries. Digital India has programs which aim to change the way, we used to deal or interact with the health services.

E-hospital is one such initiative. Aadhar card/number is a must for using this facility. It is a portal through which the citizens can book appointments in government and government recognised hospitals across the country. Not only we can fix appointments but also we can get laboratory reports, availability of blood etc.

More than 50 hospitals have been providing this facility and the number is increasing day by day. The registration process is simple. Visit this site *http://ors.gov.in/copp/appointment.jsp*. You need to register with your Aadhar number towards your identification. Select your preferred hospital, select the department, and select your preferred date for appointment. You will get a confirmation message on your mobile phone. And it's all done!

See how digitalisation of services had changed our life? You don't need to visit the hospital and run to book an appointment. You can use this facility on the go or sitting at your home or office .It can save a lot of time and money. The best thing is that people living in remote areas need not visit the hospital multiple times to fix an appointment. This is a great relief for them too. Health sector will also see further advanced methods in the coming future, which will change the traditional methods and make it more friendly and comfortable.

CHAPTER TWENTY-SIX

Digital India and its Success

There is no doubt about its success. We can see the results everywhere.See, we can actually feel the country changing because of Digital Technology.There are tremendous growth in the number of users of digital services.

The number of mobile and internet users have been increased.There is wide broadband connectivity across the country, and more and more technological improvements are happening in various sectors.

Many governmental services can now be obtained online.Earlier these services required tough formalities, days of effort, time, and delay in getting responses. Since its now being online, everyone will get these services equally and irrespective of any bias.It also saves money,time and effort.

Easy access to information is possible, and the information can be retrieved at anytime. More and more people, especially the rural population will get more communication networks and an easy access to internet and other digital services. As a result, their social and economic status will improve.

Active participation from all the 1 Billion citizens of our country is very essential factor in making this Digital India initiative a grand success.The people should forget their political views and difference in opinions and come together to join this initiative which is going to make our country a higly developed nation.

Digital India is not only going to imporve our digital and IT services but it will also make tremendous improvements in all the sectors of the economy.

Wholehearted support and activities are needed from all of us. That is the main requirement to make it more successful.Find time to educate as many people as possible about the various benefits of digital services.It will imporve the way of living of such people.As the people gets more progress, the society develops, and eventually it will develop the nation.

Awareness campaigns are very much needed even from the school level itself. Identifying areas which needs government attention should be carefully noted and infromed to the authorities.Now we can directly give our suggestions to the government through mygov.in portal and they will surely take action for it.

Active participation from all of us is very essential. Let us unite for this wonderful cause for our nation.

CHAPTER TWENTY-SEVEN

Contributions to increase National Income

It is proved that Digital India and its services contribute positively towards our national income. It transforms all our systems and sections of our economy and makes it advanced, well structured, reliable, secure, and cost effective etc. These improvements will give many advantages to different sectors of our economy. Let it be manufacturing, service or industrial sector, the Digital India and its projects will dramatically improve its services in a countless ways.

Our country gets more revenue from its service sector. And it contributes more to our GDP (Gross Domestic Product) which is the total value of goods and services produced in a country during a financial year. As a result of Digital technology, the service sector gets more systematic, innovative and advanced, and thereby the output also increases, and this leads to high growth rate and more revenue.

Our manufacturing and industrial sector will also flourish under the support of Digital India programs. Innovative methods of manufacturing goods will save time, cost and leads to creation of good quality products at affordable prices. It will also cause price stabilisation. It will be a great blessing for the potential customers as well.

A report by Deloitte, a famous IT firm says that if Digital India campaign can increase broadband penetration in the country by 50% and mobile penetration by 30% within 2 years, then this will lead to an increase in 9% in GDP. The current pace at which the programme develops, we can surely achieve this growth rate.

28. Training on Digital Services

IT literacy (Information Technology) or Digital Training means the capacity or ability to use digital services. It is not only the ability to know how to use the internet.

As a result of Digital India, more multinational tech giants have started to invest in India in a variety of digital areas which includes funds for IT training, free Wi-Fi hotspots etc. In order to be digitally literate, a person should have basic knowledge about the use of digital services and digital applications. The government is doing a good job by creating many schemes which helps to bridge the digital divide and also to improve digital literacy.

PMGDSA (Pradhan Mantri Gramin Digital Saksharata Abhiyaan) is a program which was launched in 2014.It aims to improve the digital literacy of rural population. Its target is to make around 60 million people from rural areas of states and union territories digitally literate before March 2019.

One member from each household in the rural area is selected (the member is nominated by the family members). He will be given training for using various digital services which includes computers, smart phones, tablet computers etc. They are given training for many internet based services like using emails, searching for information over the internet, digital payments, using various online government services etc. This will helps to reduce digital divide.

The course duration is for 20 hours. The course is free and the nominated person should be between the age group 14 – 60 years. The training will be given at the nearest CSC/TC (Common Service Centre/ Training Centre. The training will be evaluated by national level agencies like ICTACT, IGNOU, and HKCL etc.

Schemes like this will have great impact in the rural regions where the issue of digital literacy is a matter of serious concern, and it will improve the life and socio-economic development of the people of rural areas. Development of the nation can only happen when the rural people also gets access to various services just like those living in cities do.

CHAPTER TWENTY-NINE

Digital India and Good Governance

The youngsters are more confident that the Digital India program will contribute towards good governance. Through Digital India initiative, the government aims to make its services quick, transparent, safe, easily accessible by citizens, reliable and it tries to draw citizens closer to government and its activities.

Good governance will happen when the benefits of the government services reach the needy. In many cases the intermediaries can be eliminated and that will save a lot of costs for the citizens. Earlier, in order to book tickets for trains and flights, people used to approach travel agents, who will charge a good amount on service charges. But now people are self dependent and will book tickets using internet facilities, thus, it saves a lot of time and money.

Talking about good governance, eliminating bribing, corruption, red tape, middlemen etc will facilitate good governance. Introduction of digital services to commonly used services will give good results to achieve good governance because it will act like a bridge between the citizens and the government.

CHAPTER THIRTY

IT and Service Sector

IT and Digital India programme is having good impact on the service sector, which is a core sector of our economy.Majority of our nation's GDP (Gross Domestic Product) comes from the Service sector.So implementing new and innovative and digital systems to the service sector will contribute great benefits for the country, the government and also for the citizens.

There are many advantages to the service sector that the Digital India can contribute. It will improve the delivery of services.It will help the users to save time, money and will make the services more comfortable to perform.

Now through the use of digital technolody it has revolutionarised the entire process of government documentation system, that is one among the many benefits of including digital methods in service sector.

Majority of the people in one way or the other uses many services in a day.Let it be water connection, electricity or public transport. In all these cases, digitalisation is working wonders and digital india will further make it even more brilliant.

CHAPTER THIRTY-ONE

Service Delivery Mechanisms - E-Kranti

After the digital revolution we can see that there are tremendous improvements and positive changes happening in the service delivery areas, let it be any form of service, everything has advanced and become more efficient as a result of the digital systems. So there is no doubt about what the Digital India initiative can deliver towards the fields of service delivery.

Just take the example of our post office. Earlier when we used to send a courier, speed post or parcel, we have no idea where it has reached at a particular moment (current status). Those days are gone, thanks to the advancement in digital technology and its application in the post office sector also. We can now easily track our consignments with just an SMS. We will get to know exactly where our consignment has reached so far and when will it be delivered. All we have to do is to enter the consignment number obtained while we register our parcel at the post office. We can track the transit status online and will get a confirmation message upon delivery.

E-Kranti was started with the vision of "Transforming e-governance", and its mission is to ensure the government's wide transformation by delivering government services electronically to citizens through integrated systems by ensuring efficiency, transparency and reliability of such services at affordable cost. Over the years many methods were adopted by the state and central governments to improve the e-governance mechanisms with focus on service orientation, transparency and citizen centricity. E-Governance and E-Kranti-Electronic delivery of services are the 4th and 5th pillars of Digital India. The National E-Governance plan or NEGP acts as the foundation for these initiatives. The primary goal is to reduce the distance between the citizens and the service delivery systems. Digitalisation of various documents are adapted to access it safely and conveniently even from remote locations, anywhere, anytime.

The main focus is to make these services available to the common man effectively – efficiently – conveniently and at affordable costs.

In the coming stages of Digital India, I firmly believe that more and more enriched innovations will happen in the area of service delivery which will save time, money, and will also improve the daily living of citizens.

CHAPTER THIRTY-TWO

Communication Sector

Digital India will bring revolutions in the fields of IT and Communication Sector. These two are among the core areas which the Digital India gives more focus. IT and Communication play a crucial role in our daily life's as well as our nation's progress. So these two areas should be carefully and systematically addressed. Our country now has a strong foundation of digital infrastructure.

Majority of the people have mobile phones and have access to the internet. The coming of more and more telecom companies pushed competition to a great height that the call and data rates have gradually reduced. As a result, now the common man can also afford to use mobile phones and its services.

Through Digital India and its programmes, we will have a well connected network throughout the country. Digital connectivity not only improves communication but also plays important role during emergency situations.

Broadband Highways is one among the 9 pillars of Digital India and under this the government aims to connect 2,50,000 of villages through high-speed broadband coverage. This will give the village people better access to information and communication. Integration of various government departments using high speed networks will further will improve the way of functioning of government systems.

Nowadays due to improved weather tracking systems, the citizens get up to date weather information, which will help them to evacuate the hazardous weather conditions. Since majority of the citizens will be connected as a result of Digital India, a lot of benefits will arise to the citizens of the country.

IT and Communications plays an important role in a nation's progress. Digital India initiative has many action plans for developing various sectors.

CHAPTER THIRTY-THREE

Digital India and Multi-National Companies

Many international technological giants like Google, Facebook and Microsoft have already started various measures to support India's Digital India mission.

As a result of Digital India, Our country has now become a paradise for foreign investors.

Google launched speech recognition for India's popular regional languages like Hindi, Tamil, Marathi, Bengali etc. It helps villagers to easily surf the net and find and learn many useful things in their day to day life.

US tech giant Apple Inc. has started a manufacturing hub for iPhones in India. The plant is located at Bengaluru, Karnataka. This is a huge investment and support for Digital India campaign. It will directly and indirectly give job opportunities to thousands of people. If this gives Apple sufficient profit, then it will attract many other firms to invest and create manufacturing hubs in India. They also have included many regional languages in their iPhone keyboards so that the user can use the services in their respective languages.

The Facebook App is now allowing us to type and share things to our friend in our regional language, and it also allows us to customize the background to make it look attractive and beautiful.

Microsoft CEO Satya Nadella is planning for the initiative of Digital India programme to include an experimental technology pilot in Varanasi. They are planning to add many more things to the 'IT' field like:-

1. Improvement in Rural Internet Connectivity.

2. Digital Cloud Services for all citizens of the country.

3. Improvement in Communication and Productivity in services of the government.

4. Implementation of software like Microsoft Azure Dynamics and Office 365 to all local data centres in India to accelerate cloud innovation.

CHAPTER THIRTY-FOUR

Advantages in Preventing Crimes

Digital methods are changing the way the police force deals with crimes. They can make optimum utilisation of the digital technology to prevent crime and to track the criminals. Technology aided investigation methods are now widely popular. It helps the investigation in many ways. We have seen many incidents where CCTV captured images/ live videos of crimes playing a vital part in the investigation process. Same in the case of mobile phone locator, where a criminal's phone location gets traced and he finally gets caught.

Digital technologies make the investigation very systematic, accurate and save time too.

In case of cyber-crimes, use of Digital equipments help to locate and identify the criminals and violators in any part of the globe. Thanks to the advancements in digital technology!

In the words of American security consultant Frank Abagnale Jr. "Technology breeds crime and we are constantly trying to develop technology to stay one step ahead of the person trying to use it negatively". He said a very relevant point. We must utilise our technology to stay one step ahead from those who use it for crimes and other negative purposes.

Through Digital India, more technological advancements will happen which will give our law enforcement agencies the tools to prevent crimes and also for capturing the criminals.

It's been an incredible journey.

I had the privilege to interact with hundreds of bright young students who are the future of our country.

This is the first time that children all over the country raised their voices for what they feel and expect from Digital India – Our Prime Minister's most ambitious project which will make our country strong in digital infrastructure as well as in new and advanced technologies.

It was a great opportunity for me to discuss with these young students and collect their views and expectations of Digital India. I was carried away by the enthusiasm displayed by them the support they had given me. Everyone was so energetic to answer the questions. I feel so proud of them because they are a generation having innovative and powerful thoughts

They presented their views on Digital India in their own words. I collected their reviews, processed it and created this book.

I wholeheartedly thank each and everyone who supported me in completing this wonderful venture.

May God's blessings be with you all?

Contact

9839093003

myrichindia@gmail.com

facebook.com/drjagadeeshpillaiofficial

youtube.com/drjagadeeshpillai